AMERICA

ABROAD

An Epic of Discovery

David Radavich

D1377106

AMERICA ABROAD

An Epic of Discovery

David Radavich

Plain View Press, LLC
1101 W 34th Street, STE 404

www.plainviewpress.net
Austin, TX 78705

Copyright © 2019 David Radavich. All rights reserved under International and Pan-American Copyright Conventions. No part of this book may be reproduced or distributed in any form or by any means, or stored in a data base or retrieval system, without written permission from the author. All rights, including electronic, are reserved by the author and publisher.

ISBN: 978-1-63210-060-3
Library of Congress Control Number: 2018962418

Cover art:
Statue of Liberty courtesy of StockSnap, pixabay.com
Colorful World courtesy of fxxu, pixabay.com
Cover design by Pam Knight

We Find Healing In Existing Reality
Plain View Press is a 40-year-old issue-based literary publishing house. Our books result from artistic collaboration between writers, artists, and editors. Over the years we have become a far-flung community of humane and highly creative activists whose energies bring humanitarian enlightenment and hope to individuals and communities grappling with the major issues of our time—peace, justice, the environment, education and gender.

for the sofa inclined
with a thirst for adventure

Acknowledgements

In addition to the talented authors who read and wrote comments for this volume, I want to thank my devoted colleagues in many literary organizations for their frequent encouragement and support. They have provided me worthy examples to follow. Special thanks to my exuberant wife, Anne Zahlan, for her unfailing wit, wisdom, and generosity.

America Narratives by David Radavich

America Bound: An Epic for Our Time (Plain View Press, 2007)
America Abroad: An Epic of Discovery (Plain View Press, 2019)

In contrast to the author's more war-focused *America Bound*, this new book is a "epic of discovery" with adventures over centuries, to parts known and unknown, in all four corners of the world and even outer space.

Contents

* Titles in brackets = Ms. Liberty speaking

Invocation

Muse, let me sing
this song of national
adventure extraordinaire,

the size of the tale,
the dimensions, are huge,

the wonders
of journey fantastical.

Help me do justice
to larger-than-life ancestors,
perilous voyages over

seas and through air
east, west, north, and south,

beyond rainbows
or deserts and jungles,

vales of
the mere ordinary.

Help me find

brain and brawn
and lore and legacy

to complete my fabulous task.

Let me report on marvels
beyond history

with a mind that is cool
and dream-fired and collected.

I need support
from the supernatural

to sluice out of sloth
the narrative that has never been

told let alone enacted
except around camp-fires

after snipe-hunts

whose wings
always get away—

PROLOGUE: TALL TELLERS

Shape-Shifter

Let me introduce myself:

I am huge; I contain multitudes.

No one knows the real me.

That's because I shift shapes,
change costumes, alter my skin color
to suit the time and place

of my own choosing.

It suits me not to let you
box me in, seal me up in a tomb

of your imagination.

No, I am Protean
beyond all reckoning,

so get used to uncertainties.

I am a voyager,
Paul Bunyan, John,

any hero
you can think of,

including bunions on your feet
from too much walking.

I know those sores!

Invention is my game, and size,
and stomping around as if

I owned every place
and knew where I was going.

That's all a pose,
but most people take me

at face value,
which helps with ruse and riches.

Let me tote you along,
show you the view, the world

from atop huge shoulders
and axe-splitting

hands that pull apart
the curtains of the unrevealed,

secrets of the sealed,
I tell you, ready yourself

for a cosmic journey, pack your brain
with some fresh and friendly
clothes, come chase

my adventures
on land and over seas.

If you listen hard,
in the end you will be changed.

Uncle Sam

I suppose you think
I'm conceited.

Not really. I just overflow
with myself

spilling over the world
in every direction.

I'm yellow, white, red, and black.

I was here in the beginning,
I am newly arrived.

Somewhere I still have my papers.
But I don't have to show
you because

this is a free world
and I do whatever I want

(within the law—and sometimes
not even then.)

It's not intentional.
Just who I am, like the Mob
or the marshal over

soul and armies
and recording contracts.

Don't take it personally.

I'm just bigger and, mostly, better.

Fact of nature,
and God in His wisdom.

(Always a He—God can't be female
in occidental thought.)

There's no
limit to where I can go.

Outer space, to the moon,
I even saunter on it, scatter dust
and bring home

boulders for my friends.

That was great fun.

Also, Mars, Saturn, Jupiter,
all the planets—at this moment
I am sailing beyond

Pluto, where life changes
dramatically.

True, it can be boring sometimes,
years and years of traveling

just to say I have seen
the unvisited.

Still, it's mostly pleasurable.

That's what I live for—
pleasure, and feeling unrestrained

by anything not originating
in my own brain.

Call me stubborn
or egotistical if you like;

I know what I want
and I seek it out everywhere

with my eyes
blinking like stars.

[Ms. Liberty]

Let me get a word in!

His isn't
the only voice—

how the world
is warmed in his hands
and shaped to his purposes.

Far from it.

I know mad stories
that bubble up
from the

grieving, restless Earth.

These are not truths
men in power
would have you believe:

Natives torn from their fires,
starving, diseased fields
poisoned as if

there were
another planet,
another not-ourself

where all detritus can
somehow be
sheathed

and disposed
of without conscience.

Forgive me
for sounding so catty.

Someone must
counter
the cosmic,

weave cloth to wear
against winter.

Freedom does not
come as a thief: it must be
born in blood

and then wiped clean
and breast-fed like any relation.

Nor can it be
beaten, not merely

remote parts of the body
shackled in chains.

These are stories
he won't tell you: not
exploits,

not glorious,
not narrated around campfires.

Me he wants to
stand in New York harbor

always welcoming,
always nurturing

without pain,
childbirth or memory.

Never mind.

My job is to carry on,
remind us of life and love,

how gardens untended,
unsacrificed, become waste-lands,

how even the dead
revisit us in their sleep.

I never rise far
above Earth, beyond prospect
of falling and shattering.

Let him tell you
of stars; mine is union—

soil and storm and cleansing waters.

[Moreover]

I've got a question
for you:

Why do we
keep repeating slavery?

True, no longer
only African bodies
chained across great seas
or burning fields,

but now everywhere
humans boxed

in factories, fast-food,
cleaning latrines

and living on
dregs of the wealthy.

Slavery of
mind and spirit.

Too many women traded
as sex-cards

old men
collect for beads.

The more computers,
trips to the moon, CAT scans,
scientific experiments,
multimedia

everywhere
simultaneous eyes

this technological octopus
we call civilization,

the more
poverty and pain,

faces looking out starved
and stuttering, eyeless, wandering
a planet no longer home.

The repetition
has gone tiresome!

For centuries
the same inhumanity.

Only now
the faces become
yours or mine,

air another prisoner,

Earth stolen
like a blue pearl

that used
to sing in the sky

now
enslaved

against the dark clouds—

Back Up

Enough already
with the doom and gloom!

(It's me again.)

She can be
such a downer.

Women and slaves are one
beast, power's another.

At least on this
globe as we know it.

So as I tell my friends:
Get over it. I did not make
this world—

actually, He was
a relative, but not everyone

agrees on that point.

Oh, well.

You can't have consensus
on power: whoever has the keys
won't open the door.

Not willingly.
Not without fighting

silly wars and bitter games.

Just because
I am the biggest

doesn't mean
you don't have a tune.

I cut through
canyons, walk in huge strides,
cast a lingering shadow.

That's what I do
as an instant traveler.

Basically, I'm friendly
in a haphazard way and fond

of my neighbors:
I get in their business.

I insist on helping
people: especially you

when you need a machine.

I don't learn languages, all things
told, but apart from that
you can tell me

in your own words.

My story is one
of adventure: explorings
that matter in

a troubled world.

When circumstances
permit, I can be generous.

I have bold ancestors
that go way back

and like the sun
don't have any rivals
(except at night).

Shining's my game—
and reflecting my self all

over the world.

ANCESTORS

Youth

I, Ponce de Leon, am still searching
for the fountain of youth.

Eternally, it seems.

I thought one time
I had found it in Florida.

Many have thought so—millions
of party-seekers clustering

along beaches, trying those waters
with their toes and swimsuits

(or less), feeling the waves bathe them
in primordial movements

that might, they think,
recover the womb.

Millions of oldsters
seeking to be reborn have gone

florid to live in complexes
with spas, golf-courses, assisted

living of all kinds, garlands of amenities.

The young themselves, on whom
youth is already wasted,

drink and tan
and drink and tan,

seeking partners to enthrottle them.

None of that really
sated me.

Such waters as I seek
are not easily found. I left

my Spain in a hurry, but with time
at my back, hazardous journey

and unknown continent,
here I am,

still questing like an American
for impossible youth,

youth even the young
never find, worrying about

whether their lives
are really so pleasurable

as the posters they spy everywhere,

here I am, perhaps in your
neighborhood,

stepping into your fountain
with these sores that will not go

away. I dream of healing
rather than youth,

eternity has become
relative—like a clock whose hands

we long to hold hostage
until we're done

tasting the hearth-warm food
of this fast passage

through the forest of living
that leaves us wanting still more—

more water, more thirst.

Let me be new all over
again, let this name stand

like a poised sword
for all believers

in

only spring.

Wealth

I, Coronado, was ordained
to find gold.

Name alone crowned me
with glitter even before I began.

The New World rang
with the bells of opulence,

I only the first
to behold its sound.

What matter I died alone,
having witnessed Indians, pueblos,

Acoma, homes
of the future dispossessed?

No man can dream
as I dreamed, gold at our feet,
on every wall like sacred

tapestries
that begged to be

worshipped.

Not even Moctezuma's
cochineal, deathless red dye
of royal kings,

was as glorious,
as fabled

as the ore I sought
in cities beyond imagination.

How many miles we rode
on horseback, dust in our eyes,

hair, nostrils pallid
as death,

mesquite surrounding us

to the bottom
of the very earth.

If I had found it,
would I have told you—

the unborn,
the untraveled?

Maybe I discovered
what most I looked for:

Your eyes seeking
my story, my untold

El Dorado, where the very
glare that makes men

turn to stone

cuts away all
longing, all sorrow,

leaves a crown
that no one,
not even in dreams,
can ever take off.

Landscape

I, Sacajawea,
inhabit hills and trees,

rivers that drown
enemies,

wind that carries
smoke of our ancestors

who came up
from the ground

on their twisting grapevine
into the sun.

This I showed—some
of it—to Lewis and Clark
when they came.

Nice enough men,
not yet so bankrupt of heart
to take what was ours.

Rivers took us
to the mouth of time
and back

into history

path of storm-twisted sycamores

herons that stand like
silent warriors.

So much

have you forgotten,
sacred heart of the earth

you cut
into quilt-squares

and poisoned like startled
snakes. No wonder

I went away

to hide again
so you'd never find me.

No one knows

where I left behind
my bones.

I like it that way:
no trace can be found
except by those

who worship their ancestors,
keep the true faith,

leave Christians, so-called,
to their books they never follow.

I'll go now like
sun into rock, splitting

open the darkness.

That's why they call me
the Bird Woman:

I sing, high in the air, words
you will never know.

Empire

I, Leif Ericsson,
am the forgotten face.

No one recalls Scandinavian
empires far to the north,

north, north of Mexico,
much earlier than the European
claimants you so prize.

And who was
the first salesman?

I've got a piece of land
I'll sell you at a good price—

Greenland, in the suburbs,
not bad for wintering,

easy to get to
and along the fishy waters.

Vinland is even better
further south—almost tropical.

I have friends
living there myself.

You can reside in a gated community
with loved ones and savor all

the amenities
you could dream.

I am not making this up.

I'm the original real
estate agent,

staking claims, posting
placards, signing documents
and making it legal.

The natives
don't know what

to make of this big white dude
with the master-plan.

That's my
secret weapon: maps.

And of course self-confidence.
I know in my gut my world is better.

That's why I left
it behind

and brought it over here
as a potted plant.

These huts I built are
something new:
architecture for the magazines.

And I know stakes
and fences.

Ya, makes for good neighbors,
the kind you can trust.

I'm starting a mythic trend here—
you'll want to get in on the ground floor.

Fabric

I, Betsy Ross,
stitch things together.

Especially young countries
that don't yet know

who or what
they are.

Let's just say
I needle folks into place—
like most women.

Only this time
there's a swatch of cloth

men salute and bow down to.

It's mighty important
what colors you choose: how they

hang together
or hang separately,

one beside the other
like conqueror or neighbor.

Shapes and patterns determine,
I knew that long since.

Not everyone
has the right eyes.

And so you keep trying.

I didn't get it the first time—
wrong circles, wrong stars, stripes
that looked like whippings.

Now I think
I've caught the essence

with my thread.

It keeps spinning out nationhood,
growing plant that blooms

all three
colors at once.

Thanks to me
who only sits rocking,

remembering

extraordinary pioneers
who fought like dogs sometimes,

lay down at night
and slept

under blankets
dreamed red and blue

into stars.

WESTWARD BOUND

Passage

Our adventure
began with the sun:

No one knows the days,
the months

we spent of our lives looking
sunward, to the west

beyond
all knowing—

everything
was expectancy

staring out when we were
not stinking sick

rocking
like a barrel

in the stomach of waves
tumbling end over end without

arriving, days and months
eating potatoes

and stale bread, salted
meat torn off from the bone,

limes hoarded like
medicine,

days and months
we gathered ourselves

over waves
blue and rolling, blue

everywhere east and west,
circle of our lives

and only
heaven's lights,

a compass, a sextant,
instinct to guide us—where?—

black at night, blue
by day,

black and blue
for days and months

and the same faces lying
haggard, hapless

in the next bunk,
some we had to throw over,

horses and pigs,
good friends we made,

only the illusion
of land but aspiration

steering
into the sunset.

Some were buoyant
away from their chains,

singing, drinking,

but I
knew none

of that intimacy
among the earth-bound

plank-mates
day to day in their

horizons of joy,

I in my wonderings
kept clouds, a stiff wind
beating my hair
and flesh

for answers.

There's no declining
this adventure,

no second thought
of escape

for reckoning,

we arrive or we die,
many or few,

days and months among
primary elements,

black and blue
westward bound

and no
other way

except time and self,
sun, water, wind, old wood

aching and eyes
that know

not
where to look.

Debarking

Woman has always
focused on her suffering.

Look on the bright side, I say:
Arrival, the first-ever Thanksgiving.

Debark, take from the trees
what you need,

build fires,
make canoes, log houses,

and then settle
down by the flames.

Now it is yours.

And the king is gone: You
are your own king

 in a wilderness
with only a few feathers

to be
plucked with guns.

That first harvest was
unforgettable,

what life feels like
when it's full

and pouring out fruits

till you forget you
almost died in the crossing.

Over food and ale—platters
and tankards—all suffering is
memory, nap afterward
slips into peace.

What a rite at
the first Thanksgiving!

Our Indian friends—who wouldn't
remain so long, it was to be
our land not theirs—

brought us corn, potatoes,
the makings of bread, tarts, breasts
of turkey, guinea fowl,

what later became mince pies,
stuffing, bean casseroles,
the whole majesty

of first encounter
over that divinest meal.

I can't claim to have cooked,
but I ate, and drank, and ate again
like a dragon or diplomat,

setting down
our digesting empire,

that night was the best
sleep in years,

I scarcely turned over
and even the wife

felt her heart warmed
over odd friends
she thought she had made.

I knew better:
Don't misread your poker buddies.
Somebody's hiding a card.

But to be landed,
to have feet again, to know
trees that stay where they started,
that is a joy only

the year-long sea-torn
soil-refugee can understand,

here anchored
just this side of rocks

between the blue seas of the past
and the black wings of night
from the west,

west to inhabited jungles
that would offer us
many a torment,

but not me:

I was determined,
I was upbeat, thrilled
with the unknown

never-ending
escape.

[Rivers]

I can't tell you
how much I relish them.

Reminders of child-birth
waters, I suppose.

The surprise, the constant
turning and altering, liquid time
flowering into

undiscovered bays.

It was a carnival
our many journeyings

through the heart
of the country,

from the beginning
passage down nerve endings
into sudden corners,
only round and banked,

Indian villages here,
cliffs there, a jutting tree
or soft shore

where we alighted
and capered like otters.

Oxbows in the sun
down the blue bloodways

of the continent's dark body,
smooth and slithering.

All very civilized
in its way.

Not like the argentine ocean,
with its cold rocking and sickness,
no shore in sight,

this was downstream,
earth solid on either side,
you could arrive at any time,

Joliet, Marquette, Hennepin
setting up camp, building a fort,
bartering with natives and sleeping
in your own portable bed.

Not a bad life, all told,
living with the blue current.

I like the mix of staying
and moving on, part harvesting,
part going with relic seeds

into the swerves.

The men were more restless,
wanted to be somewhere NOW,
whereas I savored

the process,
not having to overwork,
drifting, looking, eyes
comfortable and barely unsafe.

Oceans and wars
you can have: give me

rivers that wind and wander,
cut through ridges and fields like
a dancing scythe,

carry me with you,
paddle or steam, raft
or river-boat,

down to the Mouth
where everyone celebrates
and opens

like tomorrow.

Great Divide

No one could know
how bitter, how absolute,

how unforgiving God's Earth
can be to those who

love
climbing west.

Those who challenge
the tallest peaks,

closest heaven we have
this side of living.

I mean not only the divide
between east and west
but also the destiny of rivers:

Hudson Bay, Pacific,
Gulf of Mexico.

Ascend to that tower
and you will see all destinies
run at your feet.

But then again,
you may not get home.

The Donners were not
the only emigrants to freeze
into history,

share remains of friends,
endure years of nightmares
and dead fingers.

We knew the passes
of the high Rockies as well
as any before, we were outfitted,

ready for savagery, snow,
black black night

without comfort,
blue fingers and faces

that said, "Turn back, turn back!"
echoing above tree-tops,

"Too late, too late."

No one predicts a storm
that fierce, the sky glowering
as Satan's inner lair,

ice crusting down
shocked ravines and Earth
gaping after volcanoes.

We kept together best
we could under the rock face

and prayed like converts.
Not many believed.

Days passed, supplies gave out,
the weakest cried, fell into silence.

Why was I chosen to live?

How does resurrection
arrive with torches and picks?

I could no longer walk.

We fell into their arms
as unembarrassed lovers

and the night
took our minds

into its black chasm.

Days later—a week?—
I came back to the blue air

this side of mountains
that had all

but devoured me.

The rest still lie
under the name of a pass

marked by a plaque
accusing time

of having

significance.

Edge of the World

Take me farther west—
California—
where dreams both
live and die.

Where fog hangs
over the bay, kissing
the Golden Gate,

deeper south
where sun never stops
above tiles of swimming
pools beyond stoned palaces.

Let me stay there
forever—before there were
thoroughfares, SUVs,

security systems,
marches for immigration,

riots over race,
fights against water,
poisoning of fruit fields,
wine into industries.

Let me remember
that first arrival—

rolling our way west
like the sun,

tired as a blue ox
yoked to the heavy
wagon of hopes and fears.

Ore drew me most,
gold-dust and dreams
beyond living,

no toil
or tyranny,

self baked in paradise
with a cocktail that never
gives out, grapes

hanging
succulent above,

waters that never recede.

Could heaven be
purer than mountains arched
over peaceful waters,

seals curled
on rock dumplings,

surf cresting shorescapes?

Oh, how I lolled,
long before Chinese
rail-gangs and laundries,

Alcatraz,
Disneyian hordes!

All of us thought
our lusts had been stilled—

our feet had been cut
to ribbons and our minds
to rock, but when we stood
beside the mission

looking west

at the far edge
beyond the black world,

God delivered
His promise into
our calloused hands.

Only then
could there be

freeways and mudslides,
smog alerts and Silicon vales

for a future
with no where

to go.

INTO THE NORTH

[White Wing]

My journeys to the north
have most often

been short
and not sweet.

Not driven by hopes
or dreams

but struggle, suffering.

Mostly pursued
by demons

not of my making,
unlike childbirth or dieting:

warfare, encroachment, betrayal.

There's no escaping winter
with its blind white

bitterness,

teacher of patience
and planning.

To me
the bite lingers,

wisdom adheres to
the present successfully

arrived at.

As the novelist says,
the greatest virtue is survival.

We take all the pleasure
we can in skiing,

snowshoes, ice carnivals,
wrapping our children in thick,
lustrous sweaters that
keep us

in woolen fire.

Closed in, we think
and grow, sip soothing

liquids
and heal as we can,

longing to re-grow our wings.

Outside, storms rage
like trumpets,

death calls
quickly, with no warning.

Avalanche teaches
to beware
the unexpected,

blizzards
become the stern

parents we never knew.

No wonder
I learned migration,

the still patterns of return.

Arctic Air

Ride with me now
to the far north,

sometimes by water,
mostly by sled and snow

and finally by ice,

where everything is white
white and suffering

is assumed,

wrapped
completely in furs—

the flesh of seals
and musk ox cloaks us,

whatever saviors
we can find

to provide warmth
and wisdom

of a winter
huddled like slaves

before our makeshift fires.

Every day feels
provisional,

hard-refracted in
morning by glittering sun

by night
cold as opposites,

sky against ice,
sharp horizontal truce

every direction
you look.

Somehow there are
flowers, poppies and saxifrage,

cross-dressed penguins
in crisp tuxedos,

ranging caribou, elk, moose
who seem unperturbed
except in heat,

when we are all taken
by our desires

into the madness
of pursuit,

horns against flesh.

How great that feels
wrapped in furs against

the punishing night.

Who would have thought
in priestly Québec,

where trappers
slashed through pine-brakes,

such moments open
under the skin?

I remember territory,
so much of it you became
your own gazetteer,

jotting, plotting,
asking so many questions

and revising
like a discontented
lover.

But don't mistake:
This world is white as death,

pain gnaws at the throat
breathing air,

face uncovered
against raw wind
will die.

A simple rule even
jokers can understand.

What I like most?

You know where you stand,
nature doesn't lie,
pain is never abstract,

you feel every
inch of your body.

Gettysburg

The only answer
was to take the battle
to the north.

I dreaded leaving
our homes, families,
a settled way
of life,

so much
disease and suffering,

my feet were mush and constant
ache, many of us fell onto
the flats at night

like already corpses
who longed for oblivion.

I remember the rows
of white tents

pitched
and tenuous,

sometimes preternaturally
calm as catacombs,

other times
erupting in laughter,

sweet song,
longing, diaries,

blues so deep
they could wear

uniforms of the enemy.

I was mostly
restless, walking

the lines and thinking
too much
about tomorrow.

Day came
as it would,

hotter and hotter,
a white-hot sun burned

down death on us,
one third

of our comrades
wasted charging up

that hill—Cemetery Hill
as it came to be sorely named.

I remember the whites
of their eyes, and the white

turned faces
of the fallen, pupils

aimed back into their heads
like reversed cannons.

There was nothing
I could do but

watch blood
stream across the heavens
and keep firing.

Finally we waved
our white flags

and crept down the hill
tugging and slowly rolling
into the night.

We knew it was over.

What did we learn?

Suffering doesn't always
hobble into wisdom.

The body can roll
as a hearse with no headlights.

The nurse with
the white bandage

merely hides

the deep emptying.

European Theatre

Now that was adventure
worth the name!

First the white sand
and clear sun
of North Africa,

over seas to Sicily,
which we took like a jewel

and then marched
up Rome

into history.

Everywhere huge
artifacts and thoroughfares.

Engagement
got more interesting

by the day—death
was the price some paid,

limp or eye-patch
as souvenir.

Still we were moving,
momentum carried us north

to the silver-white
peaks of the frozen Alps

and we were almost
at bull's eye.

Nowhere had I seen
such contrast—white soft

beaches, resort towns perched
over cataracts, domes with statuary,
trees pointing up to the sun,

trains everywhere,
soldiers clustering with women
curling shoulders and arms,

then these upturned
teats of Mother Earth

snowing frigid
glamour on everyone.

Finally, into the big grinder
we marched and rode
and crawled

as human sausages.

So much for glory now.

Victory we hardly thought about,
only a cold beer, nice thigh

to look at,
next cigarette,

anything
small in our pockets

still marching
without eyes and sleep

like a foreign tongue

until—

church-bells, white flags

out the window
meaning we could

go home
at last from this

endless, hellish holiday.

Alaska

Hard to imagine
battles this far north.

I prefer a cruise
along the intercontinental waterway
slick as a motorized eel.

And we bought it,
no less.

A century ago,
got a ripping good deal
with Seward and his ice-box

from the Russians.

Today you can book
tours months in advance,

watch grizzlies from a distance,

snap those picturesque
digitals and still

dance at clubs nightly
as if the fauna weren't wild.

Violence
is harder to see

here: oil spills,
seafowl dead all along

the coastline—clamoring,
flapping against the ointments
of civilization.

Stern and opposite stand
the white white ancient glaciers

about to lose their dignity
warming into wet

memories
washing every seaport

across a world without borders.

Such fights we've had over
drilling or not drilling, reindeer,
Eskimos, and the dark

hand of man

smearing the white
winterland

with his irreversible glove.

That's so much circus
to me. I want

wildness,
nothing to worry

my noodle about,
nothing to remember,

clean as
a north wind

blowing across tundra,

I want to reach
sunshine

knowing

before
the Earth breaks.

SOUTHERN CROSS

[South of the Border]

Come on down

south to the ferocity
of painted faces,

arms raised
with clubs and war-cries,

warmth in the
territory of women,

where everything
grows and opens its mouth
enclosing the world.

Sorry to be
blunt

but it's better to face
facts—nowhere

can you
hide in this sun.

Trust me,
you'll get burned

in minutes
by ripe intensity,
so don't even try blustering.

Whatever is mellow
soon turns into a golden

caricature of itself.

From the sun-baked Earth
I make ollas and urns,

hold precious
grains and scents,
the ashes

of ancestors.

I weave into bright
baskets the sacred colors

of our foremothers,

give out their contents
to unruly children.

Everyone wonders
how we proliferate so much—

blame the sun
beating like a drum,

earth yellow as maize,
sinuous dance

of secrets
singing over skin,

mask-like and frightening.

People come here
for gold,

to purify, unlock
their bodies to sensual

space where
monuments speak

in alignment
with the heavens.

The beach feels cool,
open, but inescapable sun

makes the morning
seal like stone.

Some chase after the metal
that makes men crazy, sacrifice
every vessel of blood

for ore
that glints

and then crushes
civilizations before it.

In the face of such avarice
I grow and flourish.

[Expansion]

Try being on
the receiving end
of a visit:

It wasn't long
before America spread

southward like a woman's fan—
I have one made of bone—

Cuba and Puerto Rico,
Hawaii, and then wide asea

to this
Country of Pearls

where, hot and humid,
they found us flourishing

and took as their own.

Always we've been overrun
by others wanting our coconuts,

sugarcane, timber, rice,
gifts of the rain

forest demons.

How they marvel at
water buffalo and ducks
we raise for food.

But everything
expands at the cost

of someone else,

our gold was turned into
their sovereigns,

our fields, peoples,
islands came

under the first constitution
in the region—

only not our own
government.

Our adventure
is one of resistance:

defiance, guerilla warfare
that continues to this humid day.

We are not yellow
like you think, or timid.

We know how to nurture
and stay connected,

weaving tensile
networks

across the globe.

Everywhere man thinks
he can forget us,

pay us pittance
to wrap his wounds,

clean his drawers, go where

he sends us
without questioning.

I tell you, these islands
are many and we swim together

as a school of swordfish
beyond any net

you can throw out

to contain us.

Belt-Tightening

The sun never sets
on my global interests.

From the amber of morning
till the gold of sunset,

I need to be
there, see it all.

For that reason, I wasn't
content to go south around
the Cape of Horns

(as I call them),

the long, arduous
way of commitment.

No, I prefer
quick and easy

whenever possible,
time is money, as they say.

So I set myself
to work

with my trusty axe

and man-hours past counting,
over-sized horses, slowly

slowly we carved
from ocean to ocean.

Colón to the north,
Panamá to the southeast,

Earth's girdle
unclosing between

continents like Orion's belt—

who I resemble,
they say,
in significant respects.

Bridging astride
the Caribbean and Pacific,

my handiwork sashes
the New World,

rising and falling
with the tides, bringing

seas and seasons into balance.

I don't take entire credit,
of course. Natives

slaved and sacrificed,
I oversaw and marshaled

the great machinery
of my mores

for the good of all.

Don't underestimate strength
of purpose, or enterprise.

Nature has been
put in my path to be

improved
or perfected.

The results are self-evident
and taken for granted,

but the benefits
are better

than memory

or lingering scar
across the earth-plate,

all their weight
in gold.

Skyward

Farther to the south
and much higher,

still seeking riches
and mystery

I climb to the roof
of the Andes,

undulating spine
almost

touching the clouds,
where no one

can figure out
how they settled—

by alien space-ships or just
rock-heavy burros

plodding in
thin air,

carrying the chattels
of whole villages

up here
beyond the universe.

I scarcely
can breathe.

Wrapped in yellow alpaca
I sit as the ancients

must have, smoking,
chewing, calling the pinnacle

home part of the year.

We go down, of course,
seeking goats and guanacos,
supplies, civilization,

you can hardly stay up
forever once the xanthous
beams die into
the peaks and winter

descends
with its machete.

Everyone is fire-friendly,
handing forth meat and rice,
spices, bed-planks,

drink so strong the head
dives like a falling star.

We compare boots, look each
other in the eye, march to the end

of the trail—
Tierra del Fuego—

Region of Fire,
where gold arrows shoot

across the strait
dividing everything.

End of a continent
I like to think of as my own.

On the way back,
I manage to overthrow
one president, several in fact—

what else to do?

I like to be comfortable
when I travel

and share
my warmth

with the world.

These women who bewail
their lost children

don't know
the wonders I've seen.

[Into the Jungle]

Not everywhere
is a playground for manhood.

Some places
remain
hidden, inscrutable.

Ours he misunderstood
from the beginning.

With his warplanes
he came and saw—bicycles,

pointed straw hats,
villages of old women,

and naturally
he thought we would open

like water lilies,
strange and delicate.

Beware
the bitter root!

Remember: rice paddies
sink into water to bear fruit,

jungles close
on you front and back

like women's thighs
and never let go.

Don't take
more than your share,

and don't forget
the blood you have brought.

Our quiet weapons
you could not see: holes

in the ground
covered by wattle,

snakes below, stakes
you never climb out from,

grenades hidden like ovaries
where you least expect.

We are not so yellow
as you imagine.

Male or female,
we hide in interstices,

cling like leeches
in the golden afternoon.

You don't respect
our vegetation.

Our rivers flow quietly,
with a deadly bite.

No wonder
you stayed and stayed.

We have kept many a boy
past his reckoning.

Our country
reminds you of a mother

always embracing.

Now, perhaps,
you can hear
my midwife's advice:

If he lives,
let him fathom

the eternal feminine.

TO THE RISING SUN

Dream

Help me to find
the exotic, the magical

where I can rise
out of my skin and fly almost

without wings, leaving
this tawdry world

in the dust.

Transport me now
to the East,

where everything
is red and teeming with life.

The Near East
with its slim minarets

calls us to prayer,
offers dates
and skewered meats,

lets us climb up
on camels
and sample the vast

and always victorious desert.

But most of all
I luxuriate in the red rugs

that seem to stretch everywhere—
on walls and store-fronts,

over sofas,
across canopies,

beneath
our bended knees.

And so many smells seek
to claim us full of frankincense

and musk, aromas
that conceal and invite.

No wonder Aladdin
clung to his fabled lamp:

dusk awakes phantoms, desert
seduces with mirage.

Jewel-encrusted sword
on horseback

I ride full-speed across the steppes,
bivouac in yurts, then mount

the Great Wall
into another ancient mind.

Again red everywhere,
the proud dragon

of dynasties smiles
from latticework impossibly

intricate and
somehow riveting.

I can only bow
and offer my services.

Here I feel called out
of myself, I can be pampered,
I can be executed
or shunned.

Nothing quite shatters
like that still, calm gesture
of the hand

away or toward,

angle of the dark eyes
that has not changed in millennia.

I feel unaccountably
mesmerized,

it must be illusion,

I don't seem
vulnerable stepping into

my steaming bath.

[Shogun Wife]

I can date the year
precisely when he came: 1853.

The great commodore—
I don't know what the word means,
but I relish the sound of it—

the great commodore
sailed into Tokyo Bay in order,

he said, to "open us up"
to the world.

We could do with
some coal and trade,
he assured us,

everyone would benefit.

At first we remained skeptical,
but then he came back

in 1854, this time
with more pomp and power

and we were almost
convinced.

What could we do?

The modest East
with its settled, graceful
traditions.

But I have learned
not to trust the promises
of men.

They sweep in
with red uniforms

all glittering and words
just as dazzling—

they even
seem to believe

their own schemes
for pyramids—with them

at the top.

We give them
our love, our treasure,
perhaps our first

child,
then they sail

away with their
cargoes of convenience.

I would be angrier
except in time,

over decades,
we will become ourselves

masters of tea-talk
and trade,

ply our own sea-lanes,
for a while even

be feared.

In the end, the red
sun will rise in the East.

In the meantime,
we suffer
betrayal, abandonment.

I cry out in shame
and misery,

my love
has been taken,

a rose without thorns.

Himalayas

India I escaped to
with a guide—the best way—

a sage you may have
heard of, Rabindranath Tagore,

who led me to Agra
and silent, reflective pools

of the glittering
Taj Mahal

with its pink hues
at dawn

and memories of love.

I stood
like a statue

until the hordes
drove me

into the marketplace.

Then we moved up, up toward
the roof of the world

where monks
chant

double-toned,
piercing red chambers

with their echoing voices,

and everyone learns
desirous or not.

I stare like a sinner
touring the last sanctuary,

closest to gods
any human

may venture.

They tell me, sit
on the mat like a Buddha
and clear your mind.

I meditate
like mad trying

to unfold the myriad layers
of present and past,

opening up
self as

petals of an onion.

Wow! This is definitely
not the American way—thinking.

They say, no,

you're trying too hard,
you're *working*,

it's essential just
to *be*.

Be?, I say. I'm used to doing,
accomplishing, spreading

myself
over the world.

The path inward
is the one journey I've never
taken, never attempted.

It's harder
than Everest

in the end,
and more treacherous.

Deeper
than destiny.

Slippery
as the stones

of cherries.

Iraq

It seems so strange
to find myself

again in the cradle of time,

the verdant groin
of Genesis

where it all began.

Yet here we are bringing
shock and awe

and after
a while not so much

shock, and almost no awe.

I was among the first
in, expecting

flowers, the toppling of statues.

We saw some of that,
and it did my heart good.

But these rocks
have borne so many
invasions,

good intentions
and greed

caught red-handed.

How many armies
have swept through this

birthplace of
writing, civilization?

Mongolian hordes
who looted and burned
in the sweet name of progress.

I myself believe
in democracy, the voice

of peoples
calling their senators,

pulling the levers of legislation.

Everywhere I step
someone is cowering
or shooting,

bombs explode
into hanging threads.

And so the looting continues,
treasures must be buried, we wait
for the sand to settle

scores and the remains
of empires to claim

their resting
place among pits.

Here I can't help
but learn the passing of

power from one head to the next,
ornate blood spilling out

from its red stem

into dazed fountains.

China

To go forward in time
is to go backward.

Enlightenment rises
from the East with the red

sun before its new
beginning

and day feels
full of promise

too bright
to cast any shadows.

How ancient is
this renewal, and yet

here I stand among manifold
faces unlike any masks

I have seen
painted or worn

anywhere
on this giant sphere.

Daunting as dragons,
even as I tower

over them

and seek to read
their red lacquered boxes.

How far does my power extend,
and where does it end?

I left at home
my axe, my boots

and plaid shirt. Journeying
has clothed me in new

tapestries,
ears harken to

odd sounds, eyes wait
under a pale red cherry tree

painted on silk.

Now I reach the opposite
of where I came,

opposite of who I am,

a huge ocean's handshake
away from the self,

small face

among millions just

like it, scurrying around
a hive of smoking industries.

How sweet to know
the end and yet how bitter,

the future
of our reckoning.

Over the precipice
of time

we reach
for that final fruit,

pomegranate of
fecundity

that overtakes us with
its multitudes.

Let me climb up
this mountain of history

rock after rock,

hand
into hand,

out
over emptiness,

up toward

the red
sun awakening

EPILOGUE

Circumnavigation

What landscapes, what
peoples, what monuments
have I seen!

From the four corners
of the Earth

to all quarters, all altitudes,
a rainbow of

human experience—

red, white, yellow, and black
against this blue

planet set
in white clouds

of sometime majesty.

I have sailed seas like Vespucci,
ridden trains across steppes,
portaged over rivers,
crawled atop mountains.

Every note
of suffering and joy

I have testified.

Here I am
now flying, circling
the entire globe beyond

all earlier explorers,

I have stepped onto the moon
and planted my flag,

shuttled often
to space stations and more

carrying payloads,
conducting experiments,

hooking up with cosmonauts,
even walking in orbit

as a mortal
god.

From this vantage
I can look down and see

the whole, round
jewel

of our life
set among galaxies.

How complete
I have become, how

sovereign above-ground,
a night-blinking star

before I touch down
on soil stained

by
centuries

of blood and debris.

Restless

I still am not satisfied.

I want to escape,
go further,

soar past all the warfare
and pain. Let me

voyage

beyond—to Jupiter, Saturn,
Uranus, Neptune, even Pluto—

before I am done.

Tell the wife
and friends I'll be gone

a long time, maybe decades,
they'll need to fend

for themselves.

As for me, my eyes
search always outward
to the future,

I never look
back,

never count
the repercussions,

I am freedom in
the making,

I keep striving to locate
what has never been

found
by any life form.

I want to claim it all
in a frame

I can
call my own.

[Flame]

We're still not together,
though I keep standing tall.

He promises way
more than he can deliver,

rambles with zest
then covers up his misdeeds

like a guilty
monk

afraid of his organs.

Some day I hope
we can face life together,

walk down the same aisle
keeping promises,
greeting the unbidden

in front of
our calloused feet.

So many
needs are still

raw.

Till then I am still
looking, casting bridges

over chasms,
holding the harbor

together between warships
and pleasure-boats,

feeding the multitudes,
nursing the sick,

clutching
the forgotten,

holding high
this great flame

for the next coming—

About the Author

David Radavich is a socially committed poet, playwright, and essayist. Among his poetry volumes are *Slain Species* (London, 1980), *By the Way: Poems over the Years* (1998), and *Greatest Hits* (2000). *America Bound: An Epic for Our Time* (2007) narrates U.S. history from World War II to the present, while *Canonicals* (2009) investigates "love's hours." *Middle-East Mezze* (2011) focuses on a troubled yet enchanting part of our world; *The Countries We Live In* (2014) explores inner and outer geographies. His latest book, *America Abroad: An Epic of Discovery* (2019) is a broad-hearted companion volume to *America Bound*.

Radavich's plays, both serious and comic, have been performed across  the U.S., including six Off-Off-Broadway, and in Europe. He has published scholarly and informal essays and presented in such far-flung locations as Canada, Egypt, England, France, Germany, Greece, and Iceland. Winner of numerous literary honors, he has served as president of the Thomas Wolfe Society, Charlotte Writers' Club, and North Carolina Poetry Society and currently administers the Gilbert-Chappell Distinguished Poet Series.

David Radavich
radavich@earthlink.net
www.davidradavich.org

CPSIA information can be obtained
at www.ICGtesting.com
Printed in the USA
LVHW050734281218
601965LV00001B/1/P